*for my Mother,*
*who gave me the gift*
*of a social consciousness,*
*and who taught me*
*love...*

# soulprints

the poetry of **Rusty Berkus**

*illustrated by* **Christa Wollan**

*Red Rose Press*
*Encino, California*
*1988*

*in every heart lies a poem*
   *aching to be born*
      *to echo the deepest sense of self*
         *to transmit in truth the theme of an*
            *inner life;*
               *for the signature of the soul*
                  *set down in one's own hand*
                     *is poetry*

*Rusty Berkus*

*The Poems*

| | |
|---|---|
| *Roots Revisited* | *11* |
| *Mothers* | *13* |
| *Nat* | *15* |
| *The Hill at Immaculate Heart College* | *16* |
| *Singles Bar* | *17* |
| *In the June of Her 40th Year* | *19* |
| *Kooky Karma* | *20* |
| *The 3rd Degree* | *21* |
| *Man³* | *23* |
| *One is the Only Number* | *24* |
| *Society* | *27* |
| *The Great American Self-Help Pop Psych Conspiracy* | *28* |
| *Ceremony of the Ski* | *31* |
| *Directions* | *33* |
| *The Language of Life* | *34* |
| *Letter to a Friend* | *35* |
| *Us* | *37* |
| *Kiss* | *39* |
| *One to One Recalled* | *41* |
| *The Re-education of Clark Kent* | *42* |
| *The 11th Hour* | *44* |
| *The Riddle* | *46* |
| *Gone* | *47* |
| *Old Woman, Society's Child* | *49* |
| *Arms* | *51* |
| *Progress* | *53* |
| *Thursday's Child* | *55* |
| *Conversing with Silence* | *56* |
| *The New Friend* | *57* |
| *Full Circle* | *59* |

*Roots Revisited*

I remember
a fine old house
with heavy doors
high iron gates
and miles of lawn,
hideaways
I once explored
in the house where I
was born.

I remember
my room
its window seat
covered in chintz
and high above
the crowded shelves
of a young child's world
and her magical games
in the house where I
was born.

A stranger now
to this window seat
yellowed and torn
I press my face
to the cold bleak pane
begging a glimpse
of my magical miles,
but a colorless patch
of dried-up weeds
is all that remains
at the house where I
was born.

I am transfixed
by the old iron gates
rusty and bent
the gabled roof
is not so tall
the heavy doors
are not so heavy after all
the crowded shelves
dusty and chipped
the few old books
are scattered about
in the house where I
was born.

I find it hard
the letting go
of the grand old gates
and the heavy doors
my clouding eyes
obscure the forms
of the gabled roof
and shrivelled miles.
I turn my back,
I won't look back
at the tiny house,
like a dried-up weed,
the house where I
was born.

## Mothers

*are you listening Mother*
*can you hear me*
*I talk to you of dinner tomorrow night*
*not really thinking of tomorrow night's dinner*
*I'm thinking of you.*

*we will sit at the table*
*a comfortable buffer between us*
*eating, wiping our mouths*
*instead of dabbing the tears*
*for the unsaid words between us.*

*are you listening Mother*
*I think you can read my mind*
*that you know how little I care about dinner*
*how tasteless life is*
*without the tender talking that transcends time.*
*there is still time for us Mother.*

*perhaps you wished your own Mother*
*could have read your mind*
*wanting her to get up from the table*
*put her heavy arms around you*
*to hear the tender talking that transcends*
*time.*

*I know you can't read my mind*
*I want you to hear me*
*listen my Mother, I love you.*

### Nat

*The pain of parentdeath
has passed.
I celebrate,
swaddled in sweet legacies
you left to me.*

*The pain of parentdeath
has passed.
I celebrate,
your silent songs accompany
the melodies of my rebirth.*

*The pain of parentdeath
has passed.
I celebrate
all the springs of earth-life
shared together.*

*The pain of parentdeath
does pass.
I celebrate,
for I have dreams to keep
to do you honor.*

*The Hill at Immaculate Heart College*

*You bare your green bosom to the sky.*
*Primroses dot your throat, like a colorful necklace.*
*I settle into the curve of your soft belly*
*as kites sway overhead,*
*painting the air with uneven brush strokes*

*People walk the head and foot of you.*
*The surrounding buildings*
*like thoughtful mothers*
*offer truth*
*like stern fathers*
*have expectations*

*Grand old hill baring your green bosom to the sky,*
*I have walked the head and foot of you,*
*spent days dreaming under your trees.*
*To these old buildings, like protective parents,*
*I bid farewell,*
*carrying the credentials of my culture.*

*Singles Bar*

*Singles Bar*
*where a thousand words are spoken*
*without substance*
*and a thousand words are buried*
*behind a thousand shiny faces*

*Where columns of bodies*
*stand in fragile personal prisons,*
*sipping courage from glasses*
*filled with whatever will dull the senses*

*Where corridors of bodies*
*landscape the bar*
*long enough to lose some of the loneliness,*
*fantasizing a future,*
*begging with their eyes*
*to be noticed, touched,*
*connected to*

*Singles Bar*
*where a thousand words are spoken*
*without substance*
*and a thousand tears are buried*
*behind a thousand shiny faces.*

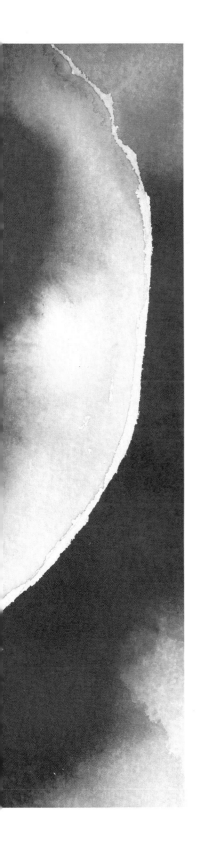

### In the June of Her 40th Year

She awakens at dawn,
pondering the position of the planets
as they play their part in the pulling
and turning of tides.
It is a day unlike all others
nothing has happened    everything has happened.
It is the June of her 40th year

She needs tending today,
rejoicing and grieving in the things done
and undone
seedlings planted long ago
sporadic sproutings
here and there
and some that never got started

How did she get here so quickly
to the center of things
this childwoman    the changing womanchild
risking reason    risking unreason
pausing to ponder "what was, what if,
what now?"
in the June of her 40th year.

How many Junes to dawn
till bouquets of beauty are gathered
into something of her person remembered?
The planet needs tending
and she wants to feel a part
of things blooming
on this day unlike all others,
the June of her 40th year.

## Kooky Karma

First day this side of January
(and all other days to come)
I get astrological around this time
I get illogical    I get maniacal
It's more of a wish thing
(witchcraft sounds too ominous)
it's more of a hope thing
(call it white magic).

I've heard Geminis are "in" this year
with good aspects in the houses of
love, money and fame.
I'll settle for one good day;
I'll settle for one great love
whom I'm destined to meet at the supermarket.

He'll be a Saggitarian
or a Gemini like myself.
The sun, moon, and stars will shine
down on us
right there in front of the freshly washed
zucchini.

First day this side of January
(and all other days to come)
lucky for me my son said,
"Mom, you never have any food in this house,"
so I scurried to the corner market
where the sun, moon, and stars were
all in alignment.
Wouldn't you know he turned out to be
a Gemini like myself.

*The 3rd Degree*

*He told her he liked women*
    *who had finished their degrees.*
*She told him she was winding up*
    *her second Ph.D.*

*He said his last affair*
    *was with a world-renowned MD.*
*She said she'd just divorced*
    *a successful MFC.*

*His mother was Magna Cum Laude*
    *and had her MBA.*
*Her dad, she said, had topped his class*
    *and was a CPA.*

*While he explained his last exam*
    *was for his DMD,*
*I looked at them and, smiling, thought*
    *"It's all BS to me."*

## Man³

shuffling through modular cities
with windowless walls
up cellular elevators
to sterile cubicles
rutted, entombed
is the Linear Man

pressed into isolation
in barren superstructure
he is a duplicated
over-directed
thing

immersed in a system
imposing
mass regimentation
writhing in rigidity
he aches

from the lush softness

of the womb

he began— a Self

now molded spindled and folded

he calls from his soundproof

cube

"I was, I am, I want to be;
can anybody hear me?"

no one answers
his silent scream
the disenchanted call of the Linear Man

*One is the Only Number*

*the Neilsen ratings came in today*
*it hasn't been much fun*
*for all those executive failures*
*who couldn't stay Number One*

*Hertz and Avis are at it*
*vying for very first spot*
*Mrs S's depressed by the Best-Dressed List*
*she didn't stay on top*

*there's nothing as sad as an old prom queen*
*staring at the midday sun*
*thinking about what once had been*
*when she was Number One*

*the Wonder of Wall Street died today*
*his sales were down this year*
*he died from a corporate cancer*
*which infected him with fear*

*beware you Wonders of Wall Street*
*feeling impotent and weak*
*when the power in your genitals*
*depends on a winning streak*

*take heed you over-achievers*
*and Little League mothers too*
*when you push too far to embody a star*
*the same might happen to you*

*One is the winning ticket*
*that's the American Way*
*One is the Only number*
*but does it really pay*

## Society

coming out party for a contessa
ten thousand dollars worth of
flowers flown in for the formal
fanfare; Porthault linens, Pre-
Columbian sculptured center-
pieces on tiny tables; men
in tuxedos and women wearing
Valentinos, and Halstons
danced gaily under the crystal
chandeliers to a thirty
piece orchestra. The posh
local eatery had an open bar
and a potpourri of sumptuous
canapes, smoked oxtail soup
stuffed crepes, chocolate
mousse and champagne. The
"A" party took place at the
height of the social season

patients immobilized
in State Mental Institutions
insufficient funds to
eradicate the filth,
disease running rampant;
people naked, left to die
in beds where linen has
the stench of urine and
feces; shock treatment
indiscriminately given as
men and women lie in
silent terror, bodies
weakened by substandard
food and inhuman treat-
ment; a sense of hopeless-
ness and helplessness is a
result of this low point in the
history of social consciousness

*The Great American Self-Help Pop Psych Conspiracy*

*Sigmund Freud is turning over in his grave*
*Chicken soup is out*
*Make way for the Great American Self-Help Pop Psych Conspiracy*
*Welcome to the "how to" culture*
*with books that boggle the mind*

*How to Stop Saying Yes When You Really Mean No*
*How to Stop Saying No When You Really Mean Yes*
*How to Stop Feeling Guilty without Really Trying*
*How to Stop Feeling Guilty without Feeling Guilty*
*Welcome to the "how to" culture*
*with books that boggle the mind*

*Born to Win, Born to Lose, Born to Cry, Born to Amuse*
*Birth without Violence, Birth without Pain*
*Rebirth without Violence, Birth without Shame*
*How to Love, How to Hate, How to Fight, How to Create*
*Up from Depression, How to Cope,*
*Down with Repression, How to Hope,*
*Welcome to the "how to" culture*
*with books that boggle the mind*

*How to Win through Intimidation*
*How to Win through Determination,*
*How to Be a Loser and Survive,*
*How to Be a Winner and Feel Alive*
*How to Have Power, Innocence, Glory, Sensuality*
*How to Deal with Impotence and Improve Your Personality*
*Erogenous Zones, Erroneous Zones, End Zones, Hormones*
*Would you believe your enzymes can set you free*
*with books that boggle the mind*

*Bookstores are meccas for psychiatry—*
*pop psych supermarket chains*
*with fast, cheap, easy answers*
*to all our neurotic pain*
*Who needs to spend ninety dollars an hour*
*when a paperback can set you free*
*Welcome to the "how to" culture*
*with books that boggle the mind*

*I'm still saying yes when I really mean no,*
*still saying no when I really mean yes,*
*still feeling guilty without really trying,*
*still feeling guilty about feeling guilty*
*Sigmund Freud might have been a better bargain*
*Make way for the Great American Self-Help Pop Psych Conspiracy*
*with books that boggle the mind*

*Ceremony of the Ski*

*hot breath of the noon sun*
*melts the snow*
*on the whipped cream mountains*
*I dare descend*
*on a hero's journey*

*hot breath of the noon sun*
*melts the ice-demons lying in wait*
*I skim the crests of snowwaves*
*like a surfer riding the curl*
*on a hero's journey*

*stretched below*
*is a giant meadow*
*beckoning me to a strange white land*
*where warriors glide in parallel turns*

*hot breath of the noon sun*
*annoints my forehead*
*with perspiration*

*my temples pound in a chant*
*for innocence lost*
*and an ecstatic self reclaimed*
*on this hero's journey*

D A strange silence signals
I pulling
R pulling
E I must go to it
C with it
T the flowing force
I perplexes
O amazes
N in its
S O
N
G
O
I
N
G
N
E
S
S

Transported to uncharted worlds
where once I was a
stranger
I am granted
entry—
entering
affirms my destiny

Supple I am
bending and rising
in the wake
of this curious current
wary
of a giant
U
N
D
E
R
T
O
W
that could drag me
under
under, yet

There is no turning back
in my becoming
to when first I heard
the strange silent signal

pulling
pulling

*The Language of Life*

*we are the first novel*
*of playwright parents*
*who published our*
*souls*
*paragraphed our*
*psyches*
*with periods*
*and exclamation points,*
*their short tight sentences*
*structured our survival.*

*we are the limited editions*
*of our playwright parents,*
*their storylines repeat themselves*
*in our dark dreams*
*where demons and angels*
*parenthesize the questions*
*that could release us*
*from the primal typeset*
*of that first printing.*

*We redraft the drama*
*of our playwright parents*
*we are the editors*
*and the distributors*
*of our own existence*
*we paste-up the revision*
*for that second run*
*affixing our copyright*
*to what was foreshadowed*
*all along—*

*we have a best seller on our hands.*

*Letter to a Friend*

*Dear friend,*
*We have held our lives unfolding,*
*you and I,*
*midwived each other's pains and passions,*
*cradled each other's fragilities,*
*bringing each other life.*

*Like children playing without pretense,*
*we let no barriers stand.*
*Most protective are the unprotected moments*
*when we are swaddled in the safety*
*of the honesty between us.*

*Nature makes love easy for those who seek*
*the simple and the straight...*
*true friendship only breathes through gentle means.*

*Dear friend,*
*we share our souls unfolding,*
*you and I,*
*bringing each other home.*

US

strangers
we
by chance
upon this planet met
traded tears and treasures
opened albums
for inspection close

strangers
we
became friends
became beloved friends
loving friends
friends who loved
each other's tears and treasures
thus becoming more
ourselves
then becoming
us.

*Kiss*

*kiss we two*
*then kiss again*
*bodies like balloons*
*lifting gently in the air*
*our tongues the velvet*
*petals of roses*
*our room a meadow*
*as the weights and weary weavings*
*of everyday*
*evaporate*

*together*
*we make a soft world*
*for ourselves*
*in a kiss*
*and kiss again*

*one to one recalled*

*it was to this quiet corner of my soul*
*you crept*
*cancelling the negatives and*
*nightmares of child past*

*it is in this quiet corner of my soul*
*I cry,*
*spilling a spring's rain*
*into summer*
*tucked away you are*
*for all summers*

*when the rainy season ceases,*
*bringing its aftercalm,*
*the legacy left to me by you*
*is that in a quiet corner of my soul*
*your essence lies,*
*through which I have found my own.*

*The Re-education of Clark Kent*

*he leaps tall buildings with a single bound*
*a Superman*
*a pillar of strength*
*caretaker of woman*
*he never sleeps*

*faster than a speeding bullet*
*he slays the corporate dragons*
*strong and silent he stands*
*the caretaker of order*
*who never sleeps*

*Superman, you cannot love or touch*
*for fear of seeming soft or sick*
*you cannot fail*
*you can't be real*
*and you never sleep*

*So many things you cannot do*
*you cannot sew or rock in a hammock*
*or give into yourself or look into yourself*
*or love yourself enough to sleep*
*you never sleep*

*Superman, you fill doctor's offices*
*with vague complaints*
*and pharmacists fill prescriptions*
*for pills to make you sleep*
*you never sleep*

*What's to become of you, my Superman*
*will you die defending a pseudo-strength*
*your humanness submerged so deep*
*that you can never sleep*
*until a final sleep*

*The 11th Hour*

*under the miles and miles of ocean*
*is the death camp*
*where whales, dolphins,*
*and other blameless sea creatures*
*reside.*

*under the giant oil slick sea*
*is the water prison*
*where gentle sea creatures are caught*
*in pollution, poison, and profit.*

*there are no wardens for these seacells,*
*no keys, no midnight express*
*as the innocent inmates swim*
*through insidious liquid doom.*

*lacking the sonar consciousness*
*of the whales and dolphins*
*we wardens of the planet*
*sleepwatch through the 11 o'clock news*
*obliterating the ecological, political,*
*and economic atrocities*
*with a flick of our remote controls.*

*we wardens of the planet*
*sleepwatch*
*while journalists and poets,*
*like the gentle sea creatures*
*rot and die in prisons*
*from China to Argentina*
*from Chile to South Africa.*

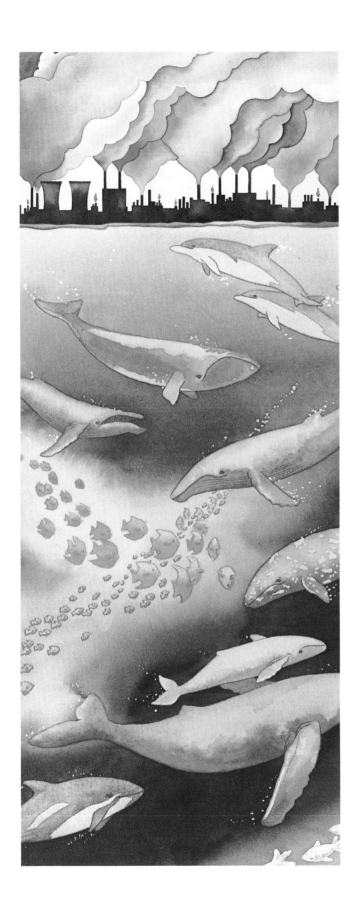

*under the miles and miles of ocean*
*up from the Auschwitz of the sea,*
*the sperm-whales, like the poets,*
*warn us of the closing clock*
*when blameless creatures beach themselves*
*to die*
*so that others might see them*
*and live.*

*The Riddle*

*In the lushest meadow of the highest mountain of Nepal*
*the old master gathered his disciples*
*and asked for the answer to the great riddle.*

*what kills people and relationships between them*
*what encourages competition*
*and causes loneliness?*

*why do people desire death rather than be wrong*
*what pulls people to glamor*
*and the accumulation of things?*

*one disciple guessed greed, another stated poverty,*
*one surmised evil, another suggested the lack of God,*
*some said conditioning, still others thought it was fear.*

*The old master smiled and said,*
*I will give you one more clue—*
*greed, poverty, evil, the lack of God, conditioning and fear*
*are all symptoms of this disease.*
*The antidote is to surrender to the path of the heart*
*or else continue to live in insanity.*

*The old master saw his disciples' puzzlement*
*and so, in the lushest meadow of the highest mountain of Nepal*
*he gave them the answer to the great riddle:*
*the disease of the soul of which I speak is that of*

*EGO*

*gone*

*the old seedlings were swept away*
                    *with the last flood*

*the daisies dried up and died,*
                    *daffodils planted in their place*

*the birch butchered, its roots yanked*
                    *to build the boulevard's bank*

*the clapboard cottage demolished*
                    *for seven miles more of freeway*

*the old park, neighborhood landmark, levelled*
                    *to raise a new market*

*the rambling highway abandoned and sold*
                    *for updated codes and fast-coming condos*

*the quiet mountain carved and flattened*
                    *for construction and crowds*

*the old seedlings swept away*
                    *with the last flood*

                    *are gone*

old woman, society's child

old woman, society's child
    who circled the dance floor with her many beaus
      led cheers for the football team
      ran for college queen
    who made love with vigor and longing
    whose hands dug deep in the earth
      as she planted seeds
        never dreamed she would someday be
            an old woman.

old woman, society's child
    who bore children
      headed up committees on those children's behalf
      raised funds for causes
      won tennis trophies, went on shopping sprees
      skied down powdery hills, took spills
    who worked off fat in saunas and spas
        never dreamed she would someday be
            an old woman.

old woman, society's child
    who sits in a convalescent home
      picks at her well-balanced plate of flat food
      wearing a housecoat bought for her
      by a well-meaning daughter
    who wins tennis trophies, goes on shopping sprees
      skies down hills, takes spills,
      and works off fat at saunas and spas,
        never dreaming she will someday be
            an old woman.

50

## ARMS

Oh beautiful
for spacious
skies
for amber waves
of grain.
For purple mountain
majesties
above the fruited
plain.
America, America,
God shed His grace
on thee,
and crown thy good
with brotherhood
from sea
to shining sea.

where are the arms to hold motherless babies
babies, who lie in their cribs
and scream
until no screams are left

where are the arms to hold the uncared-for
the old, who lie in their beds
and sob
until no sobs are left

where are the arms to hold the homeless
sleeping in cardboard
sleeping keeps them from hunger and tears
or thinking about tomorrow

can there be a tomorrow
when billions are spent
in arming for death
instead of embracing
life

do the hungry
think of Summit Conferences
the World Series
or who will win an Academy Award

do they think about Mother's Day or Father's Day
I suppose it is less hopeless
in the summertime
as opposed to Thanksgiving and Christmas
when seemingly everyone thrives on turkey
and potatoes

when one awakens with a belly pain
day after day
and there is only the energy of the sun
to warm the bones,
I don't suppose
the hungry
are thinking of Star Wars, movie stars
or the Fourth of July

in our civilized society
of electronic miracles
abundant with silicon chips, microwave ovens
and telephone answering machines,
millions of men, women, and children
awaken with belly pain
day after day

there is no energy left for anger,
but the hearts of the hungry
spill over with sadness
when all they have to taste
are their own tears

### Thursday's Child

*the gray of this day*
*holds no promise*
*of the sun barging poetic*
*through the thickness of rainclouds*

*the chill of this day*
*clings to my skin*
*like a wet raincoat*

*steelflat this day*
*I do the dance the others do*
*unsure, contrived and*
*jerkytense*
*no frills no fluff*
*no flavor*

*shall I ever see the sun again*
*barging poetic through a thickness*
*of rainclouds*
*bouncing its beams off the steelflat day*
*all frills all fluff*
*all flavor*

*Conversing with Silence*

*silence*
*my curious companion*
*I'm afraid—*
*you pull me into parts of me*
*posted with No Entry signs*
*that I alone have made*

*silence*
*my understanding friend*
*you introduce me to strange sides of me*
*those that keep me sane*

*silence*
*you steady me*
*softening my facade of face*
*where waterfalls cascade from weary eyes*
*down a trembling terrain*

*yet, yes*
*I shut out the sounds that stifle*
*unearth time in light years*
*and excavate energy*
*choosing the company of an understanding friend*
*silence*

*the new friend*

*daring to be alone in her company*
*I knew not what to expect—*
*she bid me very first thing to take leave of*
*dirty dishes, unmade beds and soiled laundry;*
*into the full sun of day she pulled me.*

*oh so loving*
*tolerant of whims*
*sensitive to my every need,*
*giving me permission to do just*
*about anything,*
*pampering me*
*expecting nothing in return.*

*as I dashed across the length of lawn*
*pretending to be a wild bird, she clapped;*
*as I read my poetry, she rewarded my words*
*with smiles and nods.*

*to think I might not have dared to be*
*alone in her company*
*(against me she could have turned at any moment)*
*it was boredom, panic and loneliness I had risked*
*when there she was for me all along*
*the very best friend in all the world—*

*myself.*

*Full Circle*

*When I grow up*
*I'll read poetry in the New Yorker*
*and it'll be okay if I don't understand it.*
*I'll not be afraid to ask stupid questions*
*or challenge authority if I disagree.*

*When I grow up*
*I'll turn down a date on Saturday night*
*if it isn't meaningful.*
*I'll even stay home on New Year's Eve*
*if I feel like being alone.*

*When I grow up*
*I might learn from listening*
*I might learn from criticism*
*I might even learn to have an "open mind."*

*When I grow up*
*I'll share all the feelings I've always*
*wanted to share.*
*I'll touch all those people I've always*
*wanted to touch.*
*I'll tell all the people I love*
*that I love them.*

*When I grow up*
*I'll go to the park and slide down slides*
*swing on swings*
*lie on the grass without a blanket*
*and make necklaces of buttercups.*
*I'll laugh at myself and giggle with others*
*scream and throw pillows when I'm angry*
*sing loudly and cry softly, cry loudly*
*and sing softly.*

*When I grow up*
*I'll forget time.*
*I'll write poetry on paper,*
*paint it on canvas or mold it with clay,*
*dance as if it were my last dance*
*and love as if it were my last chance to love*

*When I grow up*
*I'll never feel old again.*

## About the Author

*Rusty Berkus feels that in both the reading and the writing of poetry, there is a profoundly healing power. "The writing of poetry," she says, "offers each of us a great sense of psychological freedom." In her fourth book, SOULPRINTS, Rusty reveals a deeper, more personal side of herself.*

*"Poetry is the soulprint of the psyche," she says. "Through poetry, we put the gentle light of awareness on the darker side of the self. As our feelings are illuminated, we give ourselves the opportunity to experience the opening of the heart."*

## About the Illustrator

*Christa Wollan Agostino is an illustrator and graphic designer, presently working in West Los Angeles.*

*"SOULPRINTS is a book that chronicles a woman's journey of self-discovery," she says. "But even more, I find it a book about caring—for the 'little' things in life, and for the enormity of the human condition. My hope is that the images contained in this book, combined with Rusty's poetry, will inspire the reader to new depths of compassion for those who suffer; new heights of joy for those who love."*

*Acknowledgements*

*We wish to thank these photographers
for inspiring the following illustrations:*

*Page 36: Mary Ellen Mark from "The Great Themes," Time-Life, 1970.*

*Page 48: Snowden from "Snowden, A Photographic Autobiography,"
Times Books, 1979.*

*Page 52: Ken Heyman from "The World's Family," Pound Press, 1983.*

*Edited by Alida Allison*

*Designed by Christa Wollan*